Dedication

To Diane Hudson-Pappas—my partner, love, friend, and the most important other in my life.

To our sons, Julian and Brendan, in appreciation of their love and inspiration.

And to Dr. Sidney B. Simon, for his love, encouragement, trust, work in the values/human-growth area, help, sense of humor, and humility.

CONTENTS

PRIME TIME for FAMILIES

Over Fifty Activities, Games, and Exercises for Personal and Family Growth

by Michael G. Pappas
with illustrations by Karen Gundersheimer

Acknowledgments

"Things to Do" and "Time Wasters" were adapted from workshops by Dr. Blondel Senior, Ph.D., Human Research and Development Services, Inc., 2555 Madrid Way So., St. Petersburg, Florida 33712.

"Questions for Sharing" were taken from Howard Kirschenbaum's "Clarifying Values at the Family Table" in *Readings in Values Clarification*, Minneapolis: Winston Press, 1973. For a complete listing of materials available on values clarification and family enrichment, write to the National Humanistic Education Center, 110 Spring St., Saratoga Springs, New York 12866.

The "Values Goals" were adapted for use in this book with the permission of Thomas C. Wright, Inc.

Front cover photo: Freda Leinwand
Back cover photo: Betty Murphy

Copyright © 1980 by Michael G. Pappas.

Library of Congress Catalog Card Number: 79-55961
ISBN: 0-03-056672-X

Printed in the United States of America.

5   4   3   2   1

Winston Press
430 Oak Grove
Minneapolis, Minnesota 55403

FOREWORD

Michael Pappas has put together some of the most amazingly delightful exercises and games for helping children and adults look at their lives and their values. These activities have been tried out with a wide variety of families, and they *work*.

The one frustration with a book like this is that it makes you wish you could live your own childhood over—and that you had had parents who knew what Michael Pappas knows. But the next best thing is to relive your childhood with your own children. Play these games. And watch all of you grow.

Sidney B. Simon
Professor of Psychological Education
University of Massachusetts

INTRODUCTION

Prime Time for Families provides ways to improve and enhance family communication, sharing, exploring, feeling, and caring. It is aimed at helping participants build on innate individual and family strengths.

The Values Goals

The simple, safe, and fun activities in this book are based on eight basic wants and needs, or *values goals*, which affect all known behavior.

1. Affection: Getting and giving friendship and love; caring and being concerned about others; having others care and be concerned about you.

2. Enlightenment, or *knowing*: Understanding the meanings of things; being able to apply your knowledge to meet your goals; being able to learn new things and giving others the same opportunity.

3. Respect: Looking up to or admiring other people and having them do the same for you.

4. Responsibility: Knowing, as well as doing, what is right for yourself and others; being trustworthy, honest, and fair; acting according to rules that protect the rights, freedoms, opportunities, and property of all beings.

5. Power: Controlling your own behavior and having the ability to make your own choices; being able to influence others to do what you want them to do; being able to share in decisions that are made by others and affect you.

6. Skill: Learning how to do things well; doing them well; feeling like you can do them well.

7. Wealth: Having the opportunity to get the goods and services you need.

8. Well-being: Feeling healthy, happy, and good in general.

Before beginning the activities in this book, you might want to discuss these values goals with your family. What does each of them mean to each person? Which is the most important, or the least important, and why? Which goals has each person already achieved, and how were they achieved? Which goals does each person most want to achieve?

Rights and Ground Rules

As is true with all games, the activities in this book have their own *ground rules*. And it's essential that each participant have certain definite *rights*.

1. Each family member has the right to act as activity leader. The leader is the person who organizes a particular activity. He or she is responsible for reading and explaining the directions and guiding the family in doing the activity. This position may sometimes be shared among family members.

2. Each family member has the right to pass. From time to time, a family member may not wish to answer a particular question. This freedom of decision should never be questioned or argued with. Unconditionally granting it will ensure a feeling of safety that is necessary for personal growth.

3. Each family member has the right to a supportive growth atmosphere. This means that no "put-downs" are allowed, *ever*—not even those done in fun. Shoulds, oughts, and unsolicited advice are also not allowed. This might be the single most important ingredient of the activities.

4. Each family member has the right to confidentiality. Each individual has the right to decide what information about him or her can be shared outside the family. No information should be shared without a person's prior permission.

Read these rights and rules aloud and discuss them with your family. Make sure that each member understands them fully. If, as you progress, your family feels the need for additional rights and ground rules, write them here:

And, finally, *this book is meant to be used*. Don't treat it like a library book. Write in it. Bend over corners for easy reference. Leave it out for family members to look through whenever they want to. Do the activities, games, and exercises in any order you wish. By the time you've gone through the book several times, it should look and feel like one of the family!

If at any time you have any questions, or would like to consider the possibility of entering into a family/personal-growth workshop, please feel free to write me for more information:

Michael G. Pappas
PO Box 917
Tybee Island, GA 31328

I'd appreciate it if you'd include a self-addressed, stamped envelope.

Enjoy!

MEET OUR FAMILY

This book is about us, the _____
(family name or names)

family. Our names are _____, _____,

_____, _____, _____,

and _____.

We live at _____
(street address)

in _____.
(town and state)

We're a unique group of people.

> We have a lot of combined talents.
> We love and are loved.
> We understand the meanings of things.
> We are people of leadership, influence, and authority.
> We are fair people who take responsibility for ourselves
>   and others.
> We look up to one another and like being looked up to.
> We have the "can-do" spirit.
> We find the means to do the things we want to do.
> We do what we can to take care of ourselves, both
>   physically and mentally.

As you can see, we have a lot going for us!

Here is what we look like today:

(Draw or paste pictures of family members here.)

Beginnings

Our family began in _____ when _____
                          (year)   (mother's name)

and _____ first met.
      (father's name)

This is how we met: _____

_____

_____.

Here are some other precious memories we share of the

time we were courting: _____

_____

_____.

These are some of the people who were helpful to us

during that early time: _____, _____,

_____, _____, _____,

_____, _____, _____.

Our first dwelling was a _____.
                              (description of home or apartment)

It was located in _____.
                              (town)

8

We decided to live there because _____.

Here are some other precious memories we share of our

early years together: _____

_____

_____.

Since then, our family has grown to include _____,
(children's names)

_____, _____, _____,

_____, and _____.

Our Family Grows

Each child is a beautiful part of our love and our life
together. Each shares our world in a very special way.

Something wonderful we will always remember about

_____ is _____.
(child's name)

Something wonderful we will always remember about

_____ is _____.
(child's name)

Something wonderful we will always remember about

_____ is _____.
     (child's name)

Something wonderful we will always remember about

_____ is _____.
     (child's name)

Some of the people who helped us to look after our

children with love and care are: _____,

_____, _____, _____,

_____, and _____.

And now look! Look and see what fine, growing persons these one-time infants have become.

(Draw or paste a picture of children here.)

Our Family Tree

Here is what our family tree looks like:

Children

Mother	Father

Grandmother	Grandfather	Grandmother	Grandfather

Great-Grandmother	Great-Grandmother	Great-Grandmother	Great-Grandmother

Great-Grandfather	Great-Grandfather	Great-Grandfather	Great-Grandfather

Each of us helps to keep our tree living and growing and strong.

TAKING STOCK OF OUR FAMILY

Any good storekeeper takes inventory from time to time. In the same way, a family should sit down together periodically to take stock of its wants and needs, its supplies and demands. The twelve exercises in this section focus on individual and family inventories.

Exercise 1:   Kids Can Do

About the Exercise: This exercise helps the family explore alternatives for children's participation in the physical operation of the home. Getting children involved enhances their "can-do" spirit, distributes responsibilities more evenly, and recognizes them as helpful family members.

Materials Needed: Pencils or pens. (See Grid on pp. 14-23.)

The Leader Says: "Let's begin by thinking about the things we do to keep our home running smoothly. Since some of the jobs seem almost too big to handle, we'll divide them into 'micro-tasks.' A lot of micro-tasks go into getting each job done and doing it well.

"For example, getting dinner ready involves deciding what foods to fix, cooking them, setting the table, and cleaning up afterward. Each of these smaller jobs is a micro-task.

"We'll look at each job and each micro-task one at a time and check off our names on the Can-Do Grid. Then we'll spend some time talking about how we're doing and whether we should shift any responsibilities around.

"As I read off the micro-tasks from the Can-Do Grid, tell me when I name something that you already do. If there is something you do that I don't name, let me know and we'll add to the list."

13

Tasks	names					

A. GETTING DINNER READY   CAN-DO GRID

1. planning the meal
2. taking food out of the refrigerator
3. helping to prepare the food
4. setting the table
5. clearing the table
6. washing and drying the dishes
7. putting the dishes away
8. _____
9. _____
10. _____

Tasks	names						

B. CLEANING A ROOM CAN-DO GRID

1. picking up
2. operating the vacuum cleaner
3. dusting

4. _____

5. _____

6. _____

C. DOING THE LAUNDRY

1. sorting the clothes for washing
2. loading and operating the washing machine
3. taking clothes out of the washing machine

Tasks	names						
4. using the dryer							
5. hanging clothes on the line							
6. taking clothes off of the line							
7. taking clothes out of the dryer							
8. ironing							
9. folding clothes							
10. sorting clothes before putting them away							
11. putting clothes away							
12. _____							
13. _____							
14. _____							

Tasks	names						

D. TAKING CARE OF THE YARD

CAN-DO GRID

1. picking up things from the lawn

2. using the lawn mower

3. trimming the yard

4. raking leaves

5. watering the yard

6. taking care of the garden

7. pulling weeds

8. _____

9. _____

10. _____

Tasks	names						

E. TAKING CARE OF THE CAR   CAN-DO GRID

1. picking up litter
   from the inside
2. cleaning the inside
   surfaces

3. cleaning the windows

4. washing the outside

5. drying the outside

6. waxing and buffing

7. _____

8. _____

9. _____

Tasks	names						

F. GROCERY SHOPPING

CAN-DO GRID

1. reading newspapers to find out about sales
2. clipping coupons
3. writing the shopping list
4. carrying the list in the store
5. filling the cart
6. paying for the groceries
7. carrying the bags into the house
8. putting the groceries away
9. keeping a list of things that are needed
10. _____
11. _____
12. _____

Tasks	names					

G. PAYING THE BILLS

CAN-DO GRID

1. keeping the bills
   organized in one place
2. preparing the bills
   for payment
3. writing the checks
   for the bills
4. keeping track of
   cash flow
5. helping to determine
   priorities for spending

6. _____

7. _____

8. _____

9. _____

Tasks	names						

H. TAKING CARE OF THE HOUSE OR APARTMENT

CAN-DO GRID

1. keeping track of things that need to be fixed
2. learning how to fix things
3. helping to repair or build things
4. calling and supervising service people

5. _____

6. _____

7. _____

Tasks	names					

CAN-DO GRID

I. _____

1. _____

2. _____

3. _____

4. _____

5. _____

J. _____

1. _____

2. _____

3. _____

4. _____

5. _____

Tasks	names						

CAN-DO GRID

K. _____

1. _____

2. _____

3. _____

4. _____

5. _____

Questions to Think About After the Exercise

- What did you like about this exercise?
- What did you learn from doing this exercise?
- Are you doing your share of the work around the house?
- What micro-tasks are you doing now that you would like to trade for other micro-tasks?
- What new micro-tasks would you like to learn to do?
- Is everybody in our family being treated fairly? Is anybody doing too much of the work around the house? Too little?
- What changes, if any, should we make in how we're running our house?

Sign In, Please!

Our family first did this exercise on _____.
(date)

Family members who   Something worth remembering
did this exercise: about this exercise:

_____   _____

_____   _____

_____   _____

_____   _____

_____   _____

_____   _____

_____   _____

Exercise 2:   Becoming Energetic

About the Exercise: This exercise aims at helping family members to determine which activities give them energy and which ones waste their energy.

Materials Needed: (Optional) Pencils or pens and writing paper.

The Leader Says: "Let's spend some time talking about the things we do. Which activities make us more energetic? Which activities drain our energies?

"As I read the questions aloud, make a list of your answers and we'll talk about them afterward." (Or the leader can ask family members to take turns answering the questions aloud.)

Questions

1.   Can you think of five activities that help you to become more energetic?
2.   Of these five, which one usually works best for you? Why?
3.   Of these five, which one usually works least well for you? Why?
4.   Which activity do you use most often?
5.   Can you think of five activities that waste your energy?
6.   Of these five, which do you do the most often?

This exercise was adapted from Dr. Sidney B. Simon's workshops.

Questions to Think About After the Exercise

- What did you like about doing this exercise?
- What did you learn from doing this exercise?
- Were there any energy-giving activities mentioned that you'd like to try? Which ones?
- Are there any energy-wasting activities that you'd like to stop doing? Which ones?

Sign In, Please!

Our family first did this exercise on _____.
(date)

Family members who did this exercise:	Something worth remembering about this exercise:
_____	_____
_____	_____
_____	_____
_____	_____
_____	_____
_____	_____

Exercise 3: Things to Do

About the Exercise: This exercise is intended to help participants organize their time by listing and evaluating daily goals.

Materials Needed: Pencils or pens.

The Leader Says: "As we learned from the 'Becoming Energetic' exercise, we all do things that waste our energy. Sometimes it helps to organize our time by making lists of things we want to get done on specific days.
  "Let's work together to make a family list of things we want to get done. You can fill in the list with work, play, or anything else you feel you'd like to do or should do."

Name   Things to Do

_____   _____

                                _____

                                _____

                                _____

                                _____

                                _____

                                _____

Name   Things to Do

_____

_____

_____

_____

_____

_____

_____

Name   Things to Do

_____

_____

_____

_____

_____

_____

_____

Name

Things to Do

_____

_____

_____

_____

_____

_____

_____

Name

Things to Do

_____

_____

_____

_____

_____

_____

_____

Name

Things to Do

_____

_____

_____

_____

_____

_____

_____

Name

Things to Do

_____

_____

_____

_____

_____

_____

_____

Questions to Think About After the Exercise

- What did you like about doing this exercise?
- What did you learn from doing this exercise?
- Is it important to set aside time for playing as well as for working?
- Let's plan to get together the day after tomorrow to talk about how well our lists worked for us. We'll decide then whether we should try keeping daily lists for a while.
- Do you think that your goals are realistic? Do you need any help in carrying them out?

Sign In, Please!

Our family first did this exercise on _____.
(date)

Family members who did this exercise:

Something worth remembering about this exercise:

_____ _____

_____ _____

_____ _____

_____ _____

_____ _____

_____ _____

Exercise 4:   Time Wasters

About the Exercise: This exercise is intended to help participants discover and identify the kinds of activities that waste
time. It begins by focusing in on time wasters and concludes
with a search for possible solutions or alternatives.

Materials Needed: Forms for making lists—one for each participant (see suggested format below); pencils or pens.

The Leader Says: "Sometimes it seems as if we spend whole
days without accomplishing anything. We fill up our time with
'time wasters.' We probably spend more energy wasting time
than we're aware of.

"Let's work quietly for a few moments to think about the
things we do that waste our time. We'll each make a list of time
wasters and possible solutions or alternatives. Then we'll talk
about our lists."

Suggested Format:

Name:

Time Wasters	Possible Solutions or Alternatives
_____	_____
_____	_____
_____	_____
_____	_____
_____	_____
_____	_____
_____	_____

Questions to Think About After the Exercise
- What did you like about doing this exercise?
- What did you learn from doing this exercise?
- What is your biggest time waster? What are you going to do about it?
- Are there any time wasters you don't want to give up? Why?
- Was it hard to find solutions or alternatives to some of your time wasters? Which ones? Would you like some help?

Sign In, Please!

Our family first did this exercise on _____.
(date)

Family members who did this exercise:	Something worth remembering about this exercise:
_____	_____
_____	_____
_____	_____
_____	_____
_____	_____
_____	_____

Exercise 5:   Let's Do It Again!

About the Exercise: In this exercise, participants take an inventory of activities that family members have enjoyed doing together. The family has an opportunity to remember and discuss these activities and to determine if they want to do them again and when.

Materials Needed: Pencils or pens.

The Leader Says: "We've had a lot of fun together over the years. One thing we did as a family that I like to remember was _____.

"Let's think about other activities we enjoyed doing together. What about weekend trips? Holiday celebrations? Evenings? Special birthdays? Sports?
"We'll work together to list the fun activities we remember. Then we'll decide whether we should do them again—and set a date!"

Suggested Format:

Some Superfun Things We've Done Together	Who'd Like to Do It Again?	When? (possible date)
_____	_____	_____
	_____	_____
	_____	_____
	_____	_____
_____	_____	_____
	_____	_____
	_____	_____

Questions to Think About After the Exercise

- What did you like about doing this exercise?
- What did you learn from doing this exercise?
- What do you think is the most fun our family has ever had together?
- What new activities would you like to suggest we do together?
- Who'd like to be responsible for planning our next family activity?

Sign In, Please!

Our family first did this exercise on _____.
(date)

Family members who did this exercise:

Something worth remembering about this exercise:

_____   _____

_____   _____

_____   _____

_____   _____

_____   _____

_____   _____

Exercise 6:   Let's Try Something New!

About the Exercise: In this exercise, participants explore new possibilities for family fun. They have the opportunity to collectively decide whether—and when—to try an activity that the family has never done before.

Materials Needed: Pencils or pens.

The Leader Says: "When was the last time we did something new and different together? Let's spend some time thinking about activities we've never done before but would like to try doing together as a family. What about going to a new restaurant? Going camping? Working on a project together?

"As we come up with ideas, we'll list them and talk about them. Then we'll decide whether we should try them, and we'll set a date. Maybe once we do something new, we'll like it so much that we'll want to include it on a 'Let's-Do-It-Again' list."

Something New	When Should We Do It?
_____	_____
_____	_____
_____	_____
_____	_____
_____	_____
_____	_____
_____	_____
_____	_____
_____	_____
_____	_____

Questions to Think About After the Exercise

- What did you like about doing this exercise?
- What did you learn from doing this exercise?
- Which new activity should we plan to do right away? Which will take more time to plan?
- Who'd like to be responsible for planning our next family activity?

Sign In, Please!

Our family first did this exercise on _____.
                                              (date)

Family members who did this exercise:	Something worth remembering about this exercise:
_____	_____
_____	_____
_____	_____
_____	_____
_____	_____
_____	_____

Exercise 7:   My Healthy Body

About the Exercise: This exercise offers each family member a chance to consider all of the health-enhancing activities he or she engages in. Participants then share ideas and consider new alternatives.

Materials Needed: Forms for making lists—one for each participant (see the suggested format below); pens or pencils.

The Leader Says: "Let's spend a few moments thinking about the kinds of things we do to keep our bodies healthy. What about the foods we eat? Do we get enough exercise and rest? Who does something special that he or she would like to share with the family?

"We'll work quietly to list the healthy things we do, and then we'll share our lists with one another. If someone has a new idea that sounds good, we can add it to our lists."

Suggested Format:

Name:

Things I Do to Keep My Body Healthy	New Things I'd Like to Try
_____	_____
_____	_____
_____	_____
_____	_____
_____	_____
_____	_____
_____	_____
_____	_____

This exercise was adapted from Dr. Sidney B. Simon's workshops.

Questions to Think About After the Exercise

- What did you like about doing this exercise?
- What did you learn from doing this exercise?
- What new ideas for healthy activities did you learn? Did you thank the people who gave you the ideas?
- What are some things you do that aren't really that healthy?
- What new goals would you like to set for yourself?

Sign In, Please!

Our family first did this exercise on ＿＿＿＿＿＿＿＿＿＿.
(date)

Family members who did this exercise:	Something worth remembering about this exercise:
＿＿＿＿＿＿＿	＿＿＿＿＿＿＿＿＿＿
＿＿＿＿＿＿＿	＿＿＿＿＿＿＿＿＿＿
＿＿＿＿＿＿＿	＿＿＿＿＿＿＿＿＿＿
＿＿＿＿＿＿＿	＿＿＿＿＿＿＿＿＿＿
＿＿＿＿＿＿＿	＿＿＿＿＿＿＿＿＿＿
＿＿＿＿＿＿＿	＿＿＿＿＿＿＿＿＿＿
＿＿＿＿＿＿＿	＿＿＿＿＿＿＿＿＿＿

Exercise 8: My Healthy Mind

About the Exercise: This exercise offers each family member a chance to consider all of the activities he or she engages in that enhance mental health. Members then share ideas and consider new alternatives.

Materials Needed: Forms for making lists—one for each participant (see suggested format below); pencils or pens.

The Leader Says: "Let's spend a few moments thinking about the kinds of things we do to keep our minds healthy. Which activities help us to feel better and more whole? More alert? Happier? More relaxed or contented?

"We'll work quietly to list the mentally healthy things we do, and then we'll share our lists with one another. If someone has a new idea that sounds good, we can add it to our lists."

Suggested Format:

Name:

Things I Do for a Healthy Mind	New Things I'd Like to Try
_____	_____
_____	_____
_____	_____
_____	_____
_____	_____
_____	_____

This exercise was adapted from Dr. Sidney B. Simon's workshops.

Questions to Think About After the Exercise

- What did you like about doing this exercise?
- What did you learn from doing this exercise?
- Did you learn any new ideas for activities to keep your mind healthy? Did you thank the people who gave you the ideas?
- What are some things you do that aren't really that good for your mind?
- What new goals would you like to set for yourself?

Sign In, Please!

Our family first did this exercise on _____.

(date)

Family members who did this exercise:

Something worth remembering about this exercise:

_____   _____

_____   _____

_____   _____

_____   _____

_____   _____

_____   _____

Exercise 9:   Disaster Evacuation

About the Exercise: This exercise is a lesson in prioritizing objects of value. The simulated disaster evacuation presents family members with a situation in which they must leave home—maybe forever—and take with them only the most important things. The less important things must be left behind.

Materials Needed: Forms for making lists—one for each participant ; pencils or pens.

The Leader Says: "Imagine we've just found out that we have to leave home right away. There's been a disaster—maybe a flood or an earthquake or a forest fire—and we have only a few minutes to decide what to bring with us.

"Pretend we're allowed to take only one large suitcase apiece. We have to fill them with the things that are most important to us, since we may never be able to come home again.

"Make a list of the things you want to take with you. And hurry—we have only ten minutes!"

Questions to Think About After the Exercise

- What did you like about doing this exercise?
- What did you learn from doing this exercise?
- Which of your possessions is the most important to you? What makes it so important?
- Which of your possessions could you live without if you had to? What does this game tell you about material things?
- If you had the chance, would you now make any changes in your list?

Sign In, Please!

Our family first did this exercise on _____.
(date)

Family members who did this exercise: Something worth remembering about this exercise:

_____ _____

_____ _____

_____ _____

_____ _____

_____ _____

_____ _____

_____ _____

Exercise 10:   Happy Holidays

About the Exercise: This exercise gives family members a chance to discuss the things—both tangible and intangible— that they'd most like to receive from one another as gifts.

Materials Needed: A list of gift categories—one for each participant (see suggested format below); pencils or pens.

The Leader Says: "There are some gifts—like books or clothes or toys—that can be made by hand or bought in stores. But there are other gifts that can't be bought or made—like more affection or more understanding or sympathy.
   "Let's spend some time writing shopping lists of gifts we'd most like to receive. After we've finished writing our lists, we'll share them with one another and talk about them."

Suggested Format:

Name	General Type of Gift	The Specific Gift I'd Like to Receive
_____	clothing	_____
	a magazine	_____
	sporting goods	_____
	a record or tape	_____
	a book	_____
	some type of affection	_____
	some type of understanding	_____
	some type of self-control	_____
	a new skill	_____

some type of
   influence over
   others   _____
some type of
   respect from
   others   _____
a new responsi-
   bility   _____
a better feeling
   about something   _____
a healthier
   feeling   _____
_____   _____
(fill in)

Questions to Think About After the Exercise

- What did you like about doing this exercise?
- What did you learn from doing this exercise?
- Was it hard to think up gifts that can't be bought or made? Tell us about it.
- Were you surprised to find out that someone wanted a certain type of gift?
- Which gift would you especially like to give to some member of the family?
- Which of the gifts you listed is most important to you? What makes it important? Which is least important? What makes it less important?

Sign In, Please!

Our family first did this exercise on _____.
(date)

Family members who
did this exercise:

Something worth remembering
about this exercise:

_____   _____

_____   _____

_____   _____

_____   _____

_____   _____

_____   _____

_____   _____

49

Exercise 11: My Partner and I
A Marriage Exercise

About the Exercise: This exercise gives married couples a chance to explore their relationship. It focuses on mutual appreciation and self-appreciation, individual and shared interests, and individual and shared goals.

Materials Needed: Pencils or pens.

There is no leader for this exercise. Instead, both partners work together to fill in the following inventory and discuss it afterward.

We have common interests—things we both enjoy doing. Here are some of them:

1.

2.

3.

4.

5.

6.

7.

8.

9.

10.

We also have separate interests. Here are some ways in which we express ourselves individually:

Name _____   Name _____

1.   1.

2.   2.

3.   3.

4.   4.

5.   5.

6.   6.

7.   7.

8.   8.

9.   9.

10.   10.

We have some mutual friends. This creates another common bond between us. Some of our mutual friends are:

1.   6.

2.   7.

3.   8.

4.   9.

5.   10.

We also have separate friends:

Name _____   Name _____

1.   1.

2.   2.

3.   3.

4.   4.

5.   5.

6.   6.

7.   7.

8.   8.

9.   9.

10.   10.

We share many personal goals:

1.

2.

3.

4.

5.

6.

7.

8.

9.

10.

We also have individual goals:

Name _____   Name _____

1.   1.

2.   2.

3.   3.

4.   4.

5.   5.

6.   6.

7.   7.

8.   8.

9.   9.

10.   10.

It's very important to our relationship that we see each other as beautiful, worthwhile persons. Here are just a few of my partner's fine qualities:

Name _____   Name _____

1.   1.

2.   2.

3.   3.

4.   4.

5.   5.

6.   6.

7.   7.

8.   8.

9.   9.

10.   10.

11.   11.

12.   12.

13.   13.

(Be sure to fill out this inventory for each other!)

Exercise 12: Setting Family Goals

About the Exercise: This exercise will help families decide on mutual goals in three areas: physical, mental, and spiritual. It provides families with an opportunity to make plans for improvement in each of the three areas.

Materials Needed: A goals list for each family member (see suggested format below); pencils or pens.

The Leader Says: "Let's take some time to think about goals we'd like to set for our family. Maybe we should work together to become physically healthier. What about taking swimming lessons together? Or starting to jog in the mornings?

"Maybe we should work together to become mentally healthier. Should we try reading new books together? Or meditating?

"Finally, what new spiritual goals should we set for ourselves?

"After we've filled in our lists, we'll share ideas to find out which goals we should try to accomplish."

Suggested Format:

Name: _____

Physical Goals	Things We Should Do to Reach Our Goal	How Often Should We Do These Things Together?
_____	_____	_____
_____	_____	_____
_____	_____	_____

56

Mental Goals

_____ _____ _____

_____ _____ _____

_____ _____ _____

Spiritual Goals

_____ _____ _____

_____ _____ _____

_____ _____ _____

Questions to Think About After the Exercise

- What did you like about doing this exercise?
- What did you learn from doing this exercise?
- Which goals that we shared do you think are the most important? What makes them important?
- Which goals do you think are the least important? What makes them less important?
- Which activities should we start doing right away?
- Is there anybody who'd like to wait for a while before starting any of these activities?

Sign In, Please!

Our family first did this exercise on _____.
(date)

Family members who did this exercise:

Something worth remembering about this exercise:

_____   _____

_____   _____

_____   _____

_____   _____

_____   _____

_____   _____

_____   _____

THE VALUES HOME SHOPPER

About the Activity: This activity is designed to create a fun atmosphere in which family members can discover and choose their values goals.

Materials Needed: Individual mail-order forms, one for each family member (see suggested format below); pencils or pens.

The Leader Says: "We received a new catalogue in the mail today that contains all kinds of wonderful new products. Some of them make us more loving people. Some of them make us healthier. Some of them make us more responsible. You've probably never seen a catalogue like this one before!

"Let's take turns looking through the catalogue and filling out our own order forms. (Be sure to list the item you want *most* first.) Then we'll spend some time talking about the kinds of things we ordered and why we ordered them."

Suggested Format:

Name:_____

Item Name	Item Number	Quantity
_____	_____	_____
_____	_____	_____
_____	_____	_____
_____	_____	_____
_____	_____	_____

Please send the following item as my free gift:

_____   _____
      (Item Name)   (Item Number)

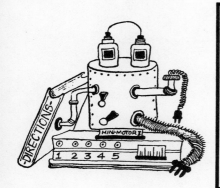

The Values
Home Shopper

Special values

for the whole family!

 Order TODAY and be eligible for this gift certificate:

THIS CERTIFICATE ENTITLES THE HOLDER
TO SELECT A *FREE* GIFT FROM OUR CATALOGUE.

From: The Special Merchandise Warehouse
        123 Values Lane
        Family Center, U.S.A.

Item #001
Basic Heart Energizer

Our Affection Department is proud to carry products that are guaranteed to fill your heart with love for others and to help you receive more love from others. Our most recent development is the Basic Heart Energizer, a sophisticated instrument that will increase the love energy output of your heart. Regular use of the Energizer will make you more loving—and more lovable!

Item #002
Size-Alike Glasses

After years of research and testing, our Respect Department is happy to present its all-new Size-Alike Glasses. When worn, these wonderful glasses will make large objects look smaller and small objects look larger. Everyone and everything will appear to be the same size! Proper use of the Size-Alike Glasses will help the viewer see material objects in a new way. In addition, the viewer will learn to respect all created beings equally.

Item #003
Mini-Motor 2

Following the amazing success of its
Mini-Motor 1, our Responsibility
Department proudly announces its
revolutionary Mini-Motor 2! When
used according to directions, the
Mini-Motor 2 will help you to do the
right things—both for yourself and for
others. It will also make you a more
honest, fair, and trustworthy person.

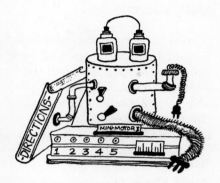

Item #004
Magic Propeller Hat

Our Enlightenment Department has a
reputation for coming up with new and
unusual products, and the Magic
Propeller Hat is no exception. Through
a patented process, this wonderful hat
pulls knowledge into the wearer's
brain. It then sorts the knowledge and
stores it in the highest layer of the
mind—where it's ready for immediate
use!

Item #005
Brain-Wave Tuner

Another great product from our Skill
Department, the Brain-Wave Tuner,
helps the wearer to develop new
mental skills by simply tuning the
receiver to the desired skill.

Item #006
Skilly Gloves

Our Skill Department has offered its Skilly Gloves for years, and they're becoming more popular all the time! Wear the Skilly Gloves and you'll be able to do tasks you never before thought possible.

Item #007
Skilly Boots

Want to run faster and farther? Want to climb mountains? Want to dance? Then you'll want a pair of our Skilly Boots—one of our Skill Department's most useful products.

NOTE: For best results, we recommend that you use the Skilly Gloves and Boots simultaneously.

Item #008
Mind-Strengthening Machine

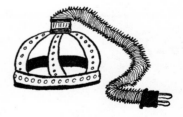

Our Power Department, which brought you the Influence-Beam Machine last year, is proud to offer its newest invention—the Mind-Strengthening Machine. This easy-to-operate device will help you to strengthen your will, self-control, and influence over others. And much, much more!

Item #009
Funny Mirror

You may have heard stories about our Well-Being Department. Well, they're all true! The people who work there are the happiest and healthiest around. And they're even happier these days, now that they're able to offer you their new Funny Mirror. When smiled into regularly, the Funny Mirror guarantees a full day of smiles, laughs, and general good humor.

NOTE: Overuse of the Funny Mirror may cause an acute case of the giggles.

Item #010
Health-Warning Buzzer

Another great product from our Well-Being Department, the Health-Warning Buzzer, is an electronic device that warns you when you are about to eat, drink, or inhale any unhealthy substance. Clip it to your collar for maximum protection. Pay attention to its warnings, and you'll be surprised at how healthy you feel after only a few days!

Item #011
Wish Package I

As you know, our Wealth Department caters to a wide range of tastes and desires. This year, it's offering three special new Wish Packages. Wish Package I offers you an unconditionally guaranteed wish. What do you most want or need? Wish Package I will make it come true!

Item #012
Wish Package II

A companion to Wish Package I, Wish Package II contains two wishes—one for you and one for a close friend or relative. Both wishes are covered by full warranty.

Item #013
Wish Package III

Wish Package III is our Wealth Department's most extravagant product. It contains *three* wishes that are *guaranteed* to come true without fail: one for you, one for a close friend or relative, and one for a person or group of people who are in need of something. You don't even have to know the person or group for whom you make your third wish. You can even use this wish for someone on the other side of the world!

NOTE: Wasted wishes cannot be traded in for new ones. And wishing for additional wishes is prohibited by law.

Questions to Think About After the Activity

- What did you like about doing this activity?
- What did you learn from doing this activity?
- Which item in the catalogue did you like best? Why?
- If you could order six items instead of five, which one would you add to your original list?
- If you could make up a product to add to this catalogue, what would it be? Which department would manufacture it?
- What did you select as your free gift? Why?

Sign In, Please!
Our family first did this activity on _____.
(date)

Family members who participated in this activity:	Something worth remembering about this activity:
_____	_____
_____	_____
_____	_____
_____	_____
_____	_____
_____	_____

LET'S PRETEND

Each of the three games in this section uses fantasy to construct a storyline and set a mood. Because these games are played in a safe family setting, members are able to explore their feelings and values without actually being threatened.

Encouraging family members to use their imaginations helps them to become aware of inner resources and capabilities that might be hidden or unused. Although it is unlikely that members will ever find themselves in the situations portrayed, pretending is a good way for them to think about how they might react in similar real-life circumstances.

Game 1: Help! I've Been Arrested for a Crime I Didn't Commit!

About the Game: This game is a test of family members' self-esteem. As they role-play the situation of being wrongly arrested, they must convince the "officer" of their innocence.

Materials Needed: A straight-backed chair, a lamp with the shade removed, and other props for an "interrogation room."

The Leader Says: "You've just been arrested for a crime you didn't commit. You know you're innocent, but you have to convince the police officer. How you handle yourself will be very important. Since most criminals have a low sense of self-esteem, the officer will be testing yours to determine whether you're guilty.

"We'll take turns role-playing the officer and the suspect. After each person has had a chance to play each role, we'll discuss what happened.

"The script is meant to serve as an outline. If you want to add anything to it, feel free."

The Script

ACTORS: One police officer and one suspect
SCENE: An interrogation room

OFFICER: Give me three good reasons why I shouldn't toss you in the slammer and throw away the key!
SUSPECT: I'm innocent! I couldn't have committed the crime because I'm _____, _____, and _____. (Name three personal qualities that you appreciate about yourself.)
OFFICER: All right, then, tell me exactly what you were doing at 8:00 yesterday evening—when the crime was committed!

69

SUSPECT: Well, officer, I'm usually doing _____ around 8:00 each evening. Last night at 8:00, I was _____.

OFFICER: Maybe you were—and maybe you weren't. Is there anyone who can prove you're telling the truth? Who will stand up for you?

SUSPECT: Someone who'll stand up for me is _____ _____.

OFFICER: What if we can't reach that person? Who else is there who'll testify that you're telling the truth about yourself? Hurry up and answer!

SUSPECT: Someone else who'll stand up for me is _____. I know that he/she would be a good character witness.

OFFICER: I'm still not convinced. What makes you think that *anyone* would stand up for you? You look like a criminal to me!

SUSPECT: Someone who knows me well could tell you that I'm _____, _____, and _____. (Name three more personal qualities that you appreciate about yourself.) A person with those qualities could never have committed the crime!

OFFICER: Well, maybe you *are* telling the truth. At least, you seem pretty sure of yourself! I'll let you go this time. You've convinced me!

Questions to Think About After the Game

- What did you like about playing this game?
- What did you learn from playing this game?
- Are there other qualities that you have that you're proud of? What are they?
- What would you tell the police about _____
(family member)

  if he or she were arrested? What would you tell them if
  _____ were arrested?
  (a friend)
- Have you ever been accused of something you didn't do? How did you feel? What did you say to convince the other person that you didn't do it?

Sign In, Please!

Our family first played this game on _____.
(date)

Family members who played this game:	Something worth remembering about this game:
_____	_____
_____	_____
_____	_____
_____	_____
_____	_____
_____	_____

Game 2: The Last Moment

About the Game: This game presents a situation in which family members are asked to imagine their last moments in life. The focus is on remembering good things about themselves and their lives.

Materials Needed: Writing paper; pencils or pens.

The Leader Says: "What if you had only a minute or so left of your life? What do you think would be your last thoughts?

"As I read you the following story, try to imagine the situation I describe. Closing your eyes will help you to imagine it more clearly.

"You're riding in a car, and your best friend is driving. As you approach a bridge, a truck enters your lane, forcing your friend to swerve into the bridge rail. The rail breaks, and the car plunges over the bridge into a swiftly moving river. Your whole life begins to flash before your eyes. You have what you're sure will be your last thoughts. Surprisingly, you're not at all afraid. Instead, you're very calm.

"As I read the next several sentences, imagine those final moments. Write down what you think your thoughts would be.

"A beautiful day I remember was when (1) _____ _____. (Pause to give members a chance to write their answers.)

"I'm really proud that while I've been alive I've (2) ____ _____.

"If I'd had more time, I would have liked to (3) _____ _____.

"I'm really going to miss (4) _____ and especially (5) _____.

"I've given a lot of love to (6) _____.

72

"One of my most cherished experiences was (7) _____
_____.

"The one picture I see in my mind right now is (8) ____
_____.

"Now close your eyes again while I read the end of the story: The dreamlike state passes as the car plunges into the river. You are knocked unconscious. Because the car is airtight, it floats to the riverbank. You regain consciousness to find that you and your friend are both alive. You may have some broken bones, though, so you don't move.

"As you wait for the rescue team to arrive, you feel relief and a deep appreciation of life and everything you love."

Questions to Think About After the Game

- What did you like about playing this game?
- What did you learn from playing this game?
- If you knew that you were going to die very soon, what are some of the things you'd do in the time you had left?
- What did this game teach you about the important things in life?

Sign In, Please!

Our family first played this game on _____.
(date)

Family members who   Something worth remembering
played this game: about this game:

_____   _____

_____   _____

_____   _____

_____   _____

_____   _____

_____   _____

Game 3: It Gives Me Great Pleasure To Introduce . . .

About the Game: This game is an activity in self-esteem and awareness of the good points of others. It gives family members a chance to appreciate themselves as well as one another.

Members are asked to imagine what they would want the host of a talk show to say about themselves. Then they are actually given the opportunity to supply the host with these comments.

Materials Needed: Writing paper; pencils or pens.

The Leader Says: "Did you know that you're a celebrity? Well, you are. And you've been asked to appear on a national talk show that focuses on personal growth. What would you like the host to say about you when he/she introduces you to the audience?

"I will read through the host's introduction, pausing for you to fill in information about yourself. Write your answers on a piece of paper numbered from 1 to 10."

The Script

"Our special guest this evening is _____.
(name)
As you all know, he/she is widely known and highly acclaimed for (1) _____. (Pause to give 'guests' a chance to write their answers.)   He/she has recently been developing in the areas of (2) _____, _____, and _____. One of his/her major responsibilities is (3) _____. He/she has spent a great deal of time learning to (4) _____. He/she recently demonstrated his/her powers of persuasion by convincing (5) _____ to (6) _____.

"Our guest has won the respect of (7) _____. In case you're wondering how he/she stays healthy, it's by (8) _____, _____, and _____.

"You may have read that _____ recently added
(name)
(9) _____, _____, and _____ to his/her material possessions. He/she is planning to add (10) _____ in the near future.

"It gives me great pleasure to introduce _____!"
(name)

"Now that we have all finished filling in the information, we will take turns being the host and the guest. The host will use the guest's information to introduce and interview the guest."

It gives me great pleasure to introduce . . .

Questions to Think About After the Game

● What did you like about playing this game?
● What did you learn from playing this game?
● What other things would you have wanted the host to say about you?
● Were you surprised by anything the host asked you during the interview?
● Was there anything you wish the host would have asked?

Sign In, Please!

Our family first played this game on _____.
(date)

Family members who played this game:

Something worth remembering about this game:

_____   _____

_____   _____

_____   _____

_____   _____

_____   _____

_____   _____

CAMPFIRE/DINNER-TABLE ACTIVITIES

Sometimes it's hard for families to set aside time for just being together. The nine activities in this section are designed to be done around the dinner table or campfire—excellent settings for family interaction. Members can talk to, look at, and listen to one another in an ideal setting for communication.

Activity 1: Plane-Crash Survival

About the Activity: This activity is designed to make participants aware of their importance within the family. With a plane-crash fantasy as a backdrop, the values goals are used to give structure to the roles that family members imagine themselves playing in such a drama.

The Leader Says: "Imagine that we're all just returning from a camping trip in the Canadian wilderness. We won the trip through a sweepstakes, and we all had a great time.

"We're aboard a chartered airplane, flying over a Canadian lake. Suddenly, one of the engines stalls. The plane begins to drop, and the pilot decides to bring it down carefully onto the lake. It hits the lake and floats for a short time before it begins sinking.

"Nobody is injured, but there's no help in sight. Luckily, there are three inflatable life rafts in the plane, and we're not far from shore. We've used up most of our camping supplies, but we have enough left for a few days of survival in the wilderness.

"What would be a good thing to do in this situation?" (Each family member should be given the opportunity to answer the question and discuss each others' answers. *Or*, the leader can ask the following questions of the group, making sure that each family member takes part in the discussion.)

"Who would be in the 'let's-get-rescued' group?

"Who would be on the food-gathering team?

"Who would be on the 'fair-share-of-everything-for-everyone' committee?

"Who would be on the 'give-some-of-my-share-to-someone-else' squad?

"Who would be in the 'let's-stay-friendly-through-thick-and-thin' club?

"Who would join the 'shelter-building' task force?"

Questions to Think About After the Activity

- What did you like about doing this activity?
- What did you learn from doing this activity?
- What other groups or teams would you suggest we add to the original list?
- In your opinion, which is the most important group? What makes it important?
- Is it a good idea to work in groups or teams? Why? What kinds of groups should we form around the house? Do we already have some groups?

Sign In, Please!

Our family first did this activity on _____.
(date)

Family members who
participated in
this activity:

Something worth
remembering about
this activity:

_____   _____

_____   _____

_____   _____

_____   _____

_____   _____

_____   _____

Activity 2:   What We Like About Each Other

About the Activity: This activity provides family members with the opportunity to acknowledge one another's good qualities.

The Leader Says: "Spend a few minutes thinking about the positive qualities of our family in general. (Pause for a minute.) Now let's focus on one person, starting with _____.
(focus person)

I'll ask each of you some questions about this person. We'll go around the table/circle so that we can all have a chance to talk about him/her. Why don't you begin? (Choose someone to begin.)

"What do you like about _____?
(focus person)

"What can you think of that's unique or special about him/her?

"What do you appreciate about him/her?

"Now tell _____ what you appreciate
(focus person)

about him/her. (Pause.)

"And that's just a drop in the bucket!"

(The activity continues until each family member has had the opportunity to be the focus person.)

What do you like about Meredith?

I like her because she listens to me.

Questions to Think About After the Activity

- What did you like about doing this activity?
- What did you learn from doing this activity?
- What other things do you appreciate about _____? About _____? Tell him/her.
- Why is it important to tell someone when we like or appreciate him or her?
- How do we feel when someone tells us that they like or appreciate us?

Tell Meredith why you like her.

I like you, Meredith, because you listen to me.

Sign In, Please!

Our family first did this activity on _____.
(date)

Family members who
participated in
this activity:

Something worth
remembering about
this activity:

_____

_____

_____

_____

_____

_____

Activity 3:   Feelings

About the Activity: This activity brings family members in touch with their good feelings and encourages them to share these feelings with one another.

The Leader Says: "When's the last time you felt really good about something? Sometimes it seems as if we don't talk about our good feelings enough. Instead, we might concentrate on our bad feelings or spend time complaining. Let's try to remember and describe the good feelings we've had during the past week. As I read the following sentences, we'll take turns filling in the blanks.

"The time last week when I felt the happiest was when _____.

"My most loving feeling was when _____.

"I wanted to help someone when _____.

"I wanted to protect someone when _____.

"I felt good about nature when _____.

"I felt good about an animal when _____.

"I felt good in a spiritual or religious way when _____.

"I felt good about myself when _____."

Questions to Think About After the Activity

- What did you like about doing this activity?
- What did you learn from doing this activity?
- What other good feelings would you like to tell us about?
- Why does it help to talk about our good feelings?
- Is it possible to feel good about something or someone else when you don't feel good about yourself? Shall we talk about it?

Sign In, Please!

Our family first did this activity on _____.

(date)

Family members who participated in this activity:	Something worth remembering about this activity:
_____	_____
_____	_____
_____	_____
_____	_____
_____	_____
_____	_____

Activity 4: I'm Glad I . . .
I'm Glad You . . .

About the Activity: This activity helps family members to appreciate their own actions and the actions of others.

The Leader Says: "Think about some things you did during this past week. Focus on the ones that made you feel good. Then think about some things that other family members did during this past week. Again, focus on the ones that made you feel good. Now we'll take turns filling in the blanks in these sentences: 'I'm glad I _____'; 'I'm glad you _____'; and 'Thank you for _____.'

"Fill in the first blank by talking about something you did. Then look at the other person as you talk about whatever he or she did that made you feel good. Then thank the person for doing it.

"We'll take turns going around the table/circle until everyone has had a chance to talk."

I'm glad I remembered grandpa's birthday. And I'm glad you are making cards to send.

Thank you for making them.

Questions to Think About After the Activity

- What did you like about doing this activity?
- What did you learn from doing this activity?
- What other things did our family do this week that deserve our thanks?
- Why is it important to thank one another for things?
- How do you feel when someone thanks you?

Sign In, Please!

Our family first did this activity on _____.
$\qquad\qquad\qquad\qquad\qquad\qquad\qquad\qquad$ (date)

Family members who
participated in
this activity:

Something worth
remembering about
this activity:

_____   _____

_____   _____

_____   _____

_____   _____

_____   _____

Activity 5: You're a Star!

About the Activity: This activity is an exercise in fantasy and imagination. It asks family members to think about movie or television characters and then decide which ones they would or wouldn't like to be.

The Leader Says: "Think for a minute about your very favorite movie or television show. Which character did you like best in it?

"Now let's go around the table/circle and take turns answering these questions:

"_____, what's the last movie or
             (family member)

television show you saw that you really liked? What was it about the show that made you like it?

"If you could be a character in that movie/television show, which one would you be? What do you think it would be like to be that kind of person?

"Which character in the movie/television show *wouldn't* you like to be? What do you think it would be like to be that kind of person?"

Questions to Think About After the Activity

- What did you like about doing this activity?
- What did you learn from doing this activity?
- Are there other television or movie characters you'd like to be? Which ones? What would you like about being them?
- Who's the worst television or movie character you can think of? What don't you like about that character?

Sign In, Please!

Our family first did this activity on _____.
(date)

Family members who participated in this activity:	Something worth remembering about this activity:
_____	_____
_____	_____
_____	_____
_____	_____
_____	_____
_____	_____

Activity 6:   Let's Eat!

About the Activity: This activity gives family members a chance to talk about the kinds of foods they like and dislike. It asks them to look at their choices from two perspectives: mental and physical.

The Leader Says: "There are foods that our minds 'like.' We want to eat them when we see them, smell them, or hear about them.

"There are foods that our bodies like, too. They agree with us and make us feel better and healthier.

"Sometimes, our minds and bodies disagree. Maybe we *want* a candy bar, but we know it wouldn't be good for our body. Or maybe we want that extra helping of mashed potatoes, but we know it'll make us feel too full.

"Luckily, there are also times when our minds and bodies agree. Let's take turns answering these questions:

"What's your favorite food?

"What does your mind like or dislike about it?

"What does your body like or dislike about it?

"When there's an argument between your mind and your body, which one usually wins?"

Questions to Think About After the Activity

● What did you like about doing this activity?
● What did you learn from doing this activity?
● Are there other foods you can think of that your mind and body agree on? Disagree on? Would you like to change any of your eating habits?

Sign In, Please!

Our family first did this activity on _____.
(date)

Family members who
participated in
this activity:

Something worth
remembering about
this activity:

_____

_____

_____

_____

_____

_____

Activity 7: Sing a Song

About the Activity: In this activity, family members exercise their creative skills by making up and singing affirmation songs about one another. They express their appreciation of one another and of themselves by giving and receiving a special song.

The Leader Says: "Maybe you've told someone in the family that you appreciate him or her. But have you ever thought about *singing* your appreciation?

"Let's use an outline to make up songs about one another. I'll start by singing a song to _____.
(family member)

Then we can take turns until everybody has had a chance to sing and be sung to.

"If you don't like to sing or don't want to do it right now, you can just say the words to your song. But this activity isn't an audition—let's have fun with it!"

Suggested Framework for Affirmation Songs:

I love _____.
_____ is loved by me.
_____ knows something about _____.
_____ has the power to _____.
_____ respects _____.
_____ is respected by _____.
_____ is responsible for _____.
_____ is skillful at _____.
_____ likes things like _____.
_____ takes care of his/her body by _____.
_____ takes care of his/her mind by _____.

Questions to Think About After the Activity

- What did you like about doing this activity?
- What did you learn from doing this activity?
- Would you like to sing a song to another family member?
- Would you like to add anything to your song?
- Let's work together to write a family song about ourselves that we can sing together. Who has suggestions?

Sign In, Please!

Our family first did this activity on _____.
(date)

Family members who participated in this activity:	Something worth remembering about this activity:
_____	_____
_____	_____
_____	_____
_____	_____
_____	_____

Activity 8:   Questions for Sharing

About the Activity: This activity is designed to stimulate thought and discussion about caring, helping, and sharing.

The Leader Says: "Let's spend some time finding out more about one another. I'll ask a question, and then we'll go around the table/circle until everybody has had a chance to answer. If you don't feel like answering a particular question, you can pass."

(Leader then selects as many questions as he or she wants to ask, or as many as are appropriate.)

The Questions
1. What is one thing you really want to do tomorrow?
2. What is one thing you'd do differently if you did today over?
3. How would your life be different if you had a million dollars?
4. What is one thing you'd like to learn how to do?
5. What is one thing you'd like to learn how to do better?
6. What was one time you really disagreed with someone today?
7. Can you recall one of the best meals you've ever had?
8. What are your three favorite main dishes and your three favorite desserts?
9. What is a funny story you heard or a funny thing that happened to you recently?
10. What is something you'd like to do this coming weekend (Christmas, summer, anytime)?
11. What was the best thing that happened at school or at work today?
12. What was the worst thing that happened at school or at work today?

13. (When on vacation) What is your most vivid memory of a past vacation?

14. (When a guest is there for dinner) What is one thing you like or appreciate about our guest?

15. (When an old friend of the family is there) What is one fond memory you have involving our guest?

16. (When an old friend of the family is there) Can you recall when and how you first met our guest and what your first impressions were?

17. (Anytime, but definitely at Thanksgiving) Proceed several times around the circle, with each person saying, "I'm thankful for . . ." or "I'm thankful that . . ." and completing the thought.

18. (At any holiday) What is the meaning this holiday has for you?

19. (At any holiday) What is your best or most vivid memory of this holiday?

20. What is your earliest memory?

21. Who is the person or character you would most like to be, if you couldn't be yourself? (This person can be from history, fiction, the news, the entertainment or sports world, a cartoon, your family or acquaintances, anywhere—real or imaginary, past or present.)

22. Who is the person (from any of the above sources) you are most like?

23. Who is the person you would least like to be?

24. What is your favorite piece of furniture in the house?

25. What is your most prized possession?

26. What is your greatest success symbol?

27. What are some of the things you'd want to do if you discovered you had only one year left to live?

28. How would your life be different if you could have one, two, or three wishes come true right now?

29. Talk about your best friend and what you like about him or her.

30. What is some change you'd like to make in your life?

31. If you could live anywhere in the world for a year, where would you want that to be? (Why?)

32. What is some question you've been wondering about?

33. Talk about anything that's been bothering you.

34. Talk about where, when, and how you learned to ride a bicycle (to whistle, to play baseball, to kiss, to dance, to write, or to do anything else).

35. What is something you feel proud of?

36. Who is (was) the best teacher you have (had)? What do (did) you like about her or him?

37. What is a social issue which you feel very strongly about? What are some of your thoughts and feelings on this issue?

38. What three things which use electricity in the house could you do without most easily? What three things which use electricity would be the last you'd want to give up?

39. What is something interesting or important you learned, discovered, noticed, or relearned today?

40. What season of the year or kind of weather do you like most? (Least?)

41. What is one thing you like better about living in the country than the city (or vice versa)?

42. What is one thing you'd like to accomplish in the coming year?

43. Where is your favorite spot to be by yourself?

44. What is your favorite book (poem, television show, kind of music, tree, flower, sport)?

45. Proceed around the table, and everyone say one word or phrase which expresses your feelings.

46. What would you like to be doing three (five, ten) years from now?

47. What is something you have in common with someone else at the table?

48. What is a quality children possess which you most wish adults would keep?

49. What do you associate with red (blue, green, yellow, or any other color)?

50. Which is your favorite room in this house?

51. What animal are you most like?

52. What is something you wish for that would help someone you know?

Questions to Think About After the Activity

- What did you like about doing this activity?
- What did you learn from doing this activity?
- Are there other questions you'd like to ask family members? If so, what are they?
- Was there a question you didn't answer that you'd like to answer now?

Sign In, Please!

Our family first did this activity on _____.

(date)

Family members who participated in this activity:	Something worth remembering about this activity:
_____	_____
_____	_____
_____	_____
_____	_____
_____	_____
_____	_____

Activity 9:   Getting to Know You

About the Activity: This activity gives family members a chance to learn more about each other through questions and answers.

The Leader Says: "We probably think that we know one another pretty well, but I'll bet there are things we *don't* know. Starting with _____,
(family member)
I'll ask a series of questions. We'll go around the table/circle until everybody has had a chance to answer each question. Then we'll discuss what we learned about one another."

The Questions

1. If you had to choose one of these places to live, which would you pick?
    - a. a house by the sea
    - b. a farm in the country
    - c. a luxury apartment in the city
    - d. a house in the suburbs
    - e. a cabin in the woods or on a lake

I want to live
on a ranch
and have a horse.

2. What kind of boat would you rather have?
   a. a fishing boat
   b. a canoe
   c. a sailboat
   d. a yacht
   e. a speed boat

3. What do you think clothes are for?
   a. to protect you from the weather
   b. to make you look good
   c. to make you feel good
   d. _____

4. What would you rather do?
   a. ride a dirt bike on the dunes and beach
   b. ride a horse on the dunes and beach
   c. ride a dune buggy on the dunes and beach
   d. walk along the dunes and beach
   e. do one of the above somewhere else

5. What would you rather do?
   a. go camping along a fresh mountain stream
   b. spend the night in a luxury hotel
   c. sleep in your own bed
   d. spend the night in the berth of a train

6. If you were going on vacation, how would you like to travel?
   a. by automobile
   b. by train
   c. by airplane
   d. by boat
   e. by spacecraft

7. Which part of the country would you most like to live in?
8. What's your favorite meal?
9. What's your favorite kind of automobile?
10. What's your favorite kind of movie?
11. What's your favorite kind of clothing?
12. What's your favorite type of beverage?
13. What's your favorite magazine?
14. What's your favorite type of book?
15. What's your favorite sport?
16. What's your favorite hobby?
17. Who's your best friend?
18. What's your favorite room in the home?

Sign In, Please!

Our family first did this activity on _____.

(date)

Family members who
participated in
this activity:

Something worth
remembering about
this activity:

_____   _____

_____   _____

_____   _____

_____   _____

_____   _____

_____   _____

FOCUSING ON OURSELVES

Many people frequently find it difficult to answer the simple question "What do you like about yourself?". It becomes easier to answer if a person looks at specific areas of his or her life. By focusing on a specific characteristic or trait, a person can grow to value that aspect of himself or herself more.

About the Activity: This activity has several sets of questions dealing with different themes. Individual family members answer the questions aloud while other family members listen attentively. You will probably want to do this activity over a number of sessions. Some sets of questions may even be alternated with other activities in this book.

The questions focus family members' attention and awareness on the speaker's positive personality traits and on the important roles that the speaker plays in the family. Besides helping the speaker focus on his or her good traits, the activity helps family members practice good listening skills.

The Leader Says: "When's the last time you thought about something you like about yourself? And when's the last time you had the opportunity to tell somebody else about it?

"We're going to do an activity together that focuses on our good points. It is very important during this activity that while one person is talking, everybody else must listen quietly and pay attention. No one should be thinking about what he or she will say when the speaker is finished. And no one is allowed to distract the speaker."

This activity and general self-appreciation techniques were adapted from Dr. Sidney B. Simon's workshops.

The Questions

Participants should choose someone to ask the questions. Each person will have one minute to answer each question.

I: SISTER/BROTHER
1. What do you remember liking about the kind of sister/brother you were when you were younger?
2. What do you like about the kind of sister/brother you are today?
3. What do you like about the kind of sister/brother you think you'll be five years from now?

II: DAUGHTER/SON
1. What do you remember liking about the kind of daughter/son you were when you were younger?
2. What do you like about the kind of daughter/son you are today?
3. What do you like about the kind of daughter/son you think you'll be five years from now?

III: FRIEND
1. What do you remember liking about the kind of friend you were to animals or to people when you were younger?
2. What do you like about the kind of friend you are to people or animals now?
3. What do you like about the kind of friend you think you'll be to people or to animals five years from now?

IV: STUDENT
1. What do you remember liking about the kind of learner you were when you were younger?
2. What do you like about the kind of learner you are today?

3. What do you like about the kind of learner you think you'll be five years from now?

V: WORKER
1. What do you remember liking about the kind of worker you were when you were younger?
2. What do you like about the kind of worker you are today?
3. What do you like about the kind of worker you think you'll be five years from now?

VI: PARENT
1. What do you remember liking about the kind of parent you were earlier in your parenthood?
2. What do you like about the kind of parent you are now?
3. What do you like about the kind of parent you think you'll be five years from now?

VII: SPOUSE OR PARTNER
1. What do you remember liking about the kind of spouse or partner you were in an early phase of your relationship?
2. What do you like about the kind of spouse or partner you are today?
3. What do you like about the kind of spouse or partner you think you'll be five years from now?

VIII: WORLD CITIZEN
1. What do you remember liking about the kind of world citizen you were earlier in your life?
2. What do you like about the kind of world citizen you are today?
3. What do you think you'll like about the kind of world citizen you'll be five years from now?

IX: AFFECTION GIVER
1. What do you remember liking about the affection you gave to others when you were younger?
2. What do you like about the affection you give to other people today?
3. What do you think you'll like about the kind of affection you'll give to others five years from now?

X: AFFECTION RECEIVER
1. What do you remember liking about the affection others gave to you when you were younger?
2. What do you like about the affection others give you today?
3. What do you think you'll like about the affection others will give you five years from now?

XI: POWERFUL PERSON
1. How were you able to use self-control when you were younger?
2. How are you able to use self-control today?
3. How do you think you'll be able to use self-control five years from now?

XII: INFLUENTIAL PERSON
1. How were you able to influence people when you were younger?
2. How are you able to influence people today?
3. How do you think you'll be able to influence people five years from now?

XIII: RESPECT GIVER
1. How did you admire and look up to people when you were younger?

2. How do you admire and look up to people today?
3. How do you think you'll admire and look up to people five years from now?

XIV: RESPECT RECEIVER
1. How did other people admire and look up to you when you were younger?
2. How do other people admire and look up to you today?
3. How do you think other people will admire and look up to you five years from now?

XV: RESPONSIBLE PERSON
1. In what ways were you responsible when you were younger?
2. In what ways are you responsible today?
3. In what ways do you think you'll be responsible five years from now?

XVI: SKILLFUL PERSON
1. How did you learn to do things well when you were younger?
2. How do you learn to do things well today?
3. How do you think you'll learn to do things well five years from now?

XVII: WEALTHY PERSON
A. 1. What kinds of material wealth did you have when you were younger?
2. What kinds of material wealth do you have today?
3. What kinds of material wealth do you think you'll have five years from now?
B. 1. What kinds of nonmaterial wealth did you have when you were younger?

2. What kinds of nonmaterial wealth do you have today?
3. What kinds of nonmaterial wealth do you think you'll have five years from now?

XVIII: PHYSICALLY HEALTHY PERSON
1. What did you do to take care of yourself physically when you were younger?
2. What do you do to take care of yourself physically today?
3. What do you think you'll be doing to take care of yourself physically five years from now?

XIX: MENTALLY HEALTHY PERSON
1. What did you do to take care of yourself mentally when you were younger?
2. What do you do to take care of yourself mentally today?
3. What do you think you'll be doing to take care of yourself mentally five years from now?

XX: SPIRITUALLY HEALTHY PERSON
1. What did you do to take care of yourself spiritually when you were younger?
2. What do you do to take care of yourself spiritually today?
3. What do you think you'll be doing to take care of yourself spiritually five years from now?

OUR FAMILY PROFILE

The activities in this book have been designed to help family members appreciate one another and themselves. By talking, listening, and sharing, we can learn to know one another better and value one another more.

As a closing exercise, family members are asked to summarize what they've learned from the various activities in this book.

About the Activity: This activity enables family members to gather what they've learned about themselves into individual profiles. These profiles can be referred to and updated as needed.

Materials Needed: Pencils or pens.

The Leader Says: "Remember when we first started using our *Prime Time for Families*? We were all a little uncertain back on page 1! We've been through a lot—and we'll be doing many of the activities again and again. But now it's time to think about the things we've learned about ourselves.

"We're going to complete a personal profile based on the eight values goals. Let's begin our profiles today and finish them over the next several days or weeks. They'll always be there to remind us of what valuable people we are."

Suggested Format:

Name _____

Date Begun _____

Affection

The people I like:

The people I love:

The animals I like or love:

The people who like me:

The people who love me:

The animals that like, love, or depend on me:

Other things I love:

Enlightenment

People I understand:

People who understand me:

Things I understand the meanings of:

How I apply my knowledge to meet my goals:

New things I'm learning:

Things I'm teaching others or helping others to learn:

Skill

My physical skills:

My mental skills:

My spiritual skills:

Physical skills I'm acquiring:

Mental skills I'm acquiring:

Spiritual skills I'm acquiring:

Respect

People I respect:

Things I respect about myself:

People who respect me:

Things about me that other people respect:

Power

Ways in which I exercise self-control:

Good choices (decisions) I've made in my life:

People I have an influence on:

People who have an influence on me:

Wealth

My favorite possessions:

My necessary possessions:

Some things that I would like to acquire:

Responsibility

Ways in which I've earned other people's trust:

Ways in which other people have earned my trust:

Ways in which I protect the rights of others:

Ways in which others protect my rights:

Ways in which I exercise responsibility:

Well-Being

Ways in which I maintain my physical health:

Ways in which I maintain my mental health:

Ways in which I maintain my spiritual health: